The

By

KAREN ZACARÍAS

Dramatic Publishing Company
Woodstock, Illinois • Australia • New Zealand • South Africa

*** NOTICE ***

IMPORTANT BILLING AND CREDIT REQUIREMENTS

The Book Club Play

CHARACTERS

ANA SMITH (w): 30s. Pronounced "Ah-nuh." Beautiful. Charming. Smart. Accomplished. Organized. A columnist for a daily paper. The "Mother Bee." Her grace masks a need to control.

ROBERT NOVUM SMITH JR (m): 30s. ANA's golden-boy handsome, charismatic, underachiever husband who is starting to search for meaning. Met in college. Upper-crust background.

WILLIAM LEE NOTHNAGEL (m): 30s. ROB's conservative, well-read, well-dressed, disciplined college roommate. ANA's former boyfriend. History buff. Unmarried.

JENNIFER McCLINTOCK (w): 30s. ANA's friend. Pretty. Shy. Smart. Tends to burst out with awkward truthful comments. Despite some lack of self-confidence, she is the grounding center of the group. Unorganized and oblivious to her own attractiveness. Unmarried.

LILY LOUISE JACKSON (w): black, 20s. A go-getter. Former debate captain who is on the cusp of all current trends and yet can still put her foot in her mouth in social occasions. Laughs at appropriate and inappropriate times. A great lover of books and ANA's protégé at the paper.

ALEX (m): 30s. The new guy. A very smart, well-read academic who has lost his moorings and is searching for real connection. Professor of comparative literature.

PUNDIT (either): plays five characters: SAM, Wal-Mart guy; FRANK, Secret Service agent; ELSA, jaded literary agent; MRS. SIMPSON, sky diver; CARL, inmate book dealer.

CHARACTER NOTES

Pace and flow is vital for this play.

For professional productions: Double the roles, using only six actors. The PUNDITS can be played by the following characters with fast minimal costume changes (one or two articles at most):

> ELSA, jaded literary agent- played by JEN
> FRANK, Secret Service agent- played by WILL
> SAM, Wal-Mart guy- played by ROB
> CARL, inmate book dealer- played by ALEX
> MRS. SIMPSON, sky diver- played by LILY

If you are using a seventh actor for all the PUNDITS, then a fuller transformation can occur, so long as the pace and flow is unaffected. The seventh actor MUST play all the PUNDIT roles as written, man or woman.

For non-professional productions: The cast can be expanded to 11 actors by having each of the PUNDIT roles played individually.

CASTING NOTE

ALEX can be cast in any race or ethnicity. LILY must be black. ANA, JEN, WILL and ROB can be any race or ethnicity except black.

SETTING

A living room in the United States circa now.

PRODUCTION NOTES

This play is stylized like a film documentary. The characters know that they are being filmed but forget sometimes.

Names of the experts and titles of the books should be projected, but all the roles, including the pundits, should be live. All the dialogue should be spoken by live actors, not filmed. The set-up is a film documentary, but the language is theatrical.

This is not a farce; it is a play about real people. The funny should come from the humanity of the characters.

DISCUSSION AND ENGAGEMENT

The Book Club Play is as much about connection as it is about books. Theatre patrons could write their favorite book on an adhesive name tag as they walk into the theatre and wear it during the play to spark discussion during intermission. At the end of the performance, the stickers could be placed on a banner when they leave, so that people can see and discuss the books others have read. Book drives and video "confessionals" of reading pleasures to "Lars Knudsen" are all various easy ways to engage audiences in discussing books before and after the play.

The Book Club Play

ACT I

***(Projection:* The Book Club: A Documentary.**

Spotlight: ANA SMITH [name flashes on screen].)

ANA. And my idea for Book Club was, simply, why don't I start a club where we all read books … together! I came up with it a good sixteen months before Oprah. Connection. Bridges. Revelation … all of those were part of my impetus to start the Book Club. Book Club is a safe haven … a place to read, talk and to be our authentic selves *(Beat.)* Was that OK? I'm happy to do it over again if you want it better.

(Spotlight: LILY LOUISE JACKSON [name flashes on screen].)

LILY. Why Book Club? Well, I like to read. I'm a writer … although, right now I'm more of an editor and fact-finder at the *Herald*. Ana, who's a columnist at the paper, invited me to Book Club. To come every month and hang with her and her old—not "old" old, but you know … longtime mature-age type friends. I just moved here to start the job and I don't know anyone, so I didn't really have a good excuse for not coming. So, why not Book Club?

(Spotlight: ROBERT NOVUM SMITH JR. [name flashes on screen].)

ROB. My wife, Ana, and my best friend, Will, started Book Club way back. I don't think they even asked me to join; it was kind of assumed I would be there. I'm not a particular big reader. But I like being around great people. I like being around good food. And it usually happens at my house. So I'm already there. I guess Book Club just sort of happened to me.

(Spotlight: JENNIFER McCLINTOCK [name flashes on screen].)

JEN. Books are like best friends to me. Truth be told, I like books more than I like most people. I'm a paralegal at a law firm where I deal with the "fine print," and angry clients, and stressed out attorneys. Book Club is a place that reminds me of the better parts of being human. It is the only place in my life where the idea of community really thrives. I truly believe a good book and a good friend can bring out the best in a person. Even me.

(Spotlight: WILLIAM LEE NOTHNAGEL [name flashes on screen].)

WILL. I simply adore books. I seriously considered getting a master's in library science, but the whole idea of letting other people take home books I had so carefully tended and organized, distressed me. Book Club is the best of two worlds. I share what I have read with people that I like, but then I take my own beautiful book home with me.

(Projection: Moby Dick by Herman Melville.

ANA, ROB, WILL and LILY are all downstage looking at the audience.)

ANA *(looking at her watch)*. OK. People. Places! Places! It's almost time. Five-four-three-two-Red light! It's on! It's on!

ROB. That's amazing!

ANA *(clears her throat, to the camera)*. Hello there. I am Ana Smith. Although you might recognize me … from my picture byline for my "Connections" column in the style section of the *Herald*, I am here in a very different role.

ROB. This is so weird.

WILL. Shhh.

ANA. And I am surrounded by some very special people Rob, Lily, Will—say hello!

LILY & WILL. Hello.

ANA. Rob, honey—Say hello.

ROB. To who? Nobody's there.

ANA. Please say hello to the camera, dear.

ROB. Hello.

ANA. This wonderful man is my husband: Robert Novum Smith Jr.

And this is Lily. This amazing, hip young woman just moved from …

LILY. Akron, Ohio

ANA. Lily is an assistant editor at the *Herald*.

LILY. Thanks to Ana, I've also written some short opinion pieces for the metro section.

ANA. Oh Lily, I see a slightly younger me in you! It's so fun to hang outside of work.

LILY. It sure is, Ana.

WILL. Salutations.

ANA. This is William Lee Nothnagel the third. Our first member and our dearest friend.

WILL. I am curator of Greek antiquities at the history museum.

ANA. And one of the best dressed and best read men that I know.

WILL. Brooks Brothers and a good book, what could be better?

ANA *(turns to the audience)*. This is most of my Book Club. TA-DA

(JEN walks in late, harried, and still reading Moby Dick.*)*

ANA *(cont'd, introduces her)*. Jennifer Mclintock … an old childhood friend of Will's and now a longtime cherished Book Club member.

JEN. Good God Jupiter, is that the … thingy?

LILY. It's moving.

ANA. It's focusing … It has a sensor that detects movement. *(Some of the Book Clubbers test it by moving.)* From seven p.m. to midnight its records everything from here to here.

JEN. Really?

ANA. Yes. Jen. Seven p.m. Sharp.

LILY. Amazing.

ANA. This state of the art camera is transmitting images to … none other than the documentary director Lars Knudsen.

JEN. Lars Knudsen!?

WILL. I can't believe this! Lars Knudsen!

LILY. I loved his film *Hard Hats*.

WILL. Mesmerizing! It was all about construction workers in Canada.

ROB. Who is Lars—

ANA. KNUDSEN?

LILY. He is a cutting edge documentary director from Denmark whose work captures the essence of humanity by unobtrusively filming real people going about their real lives in real time.

ANA. And our Danish director is focusing on the American phenomenon of Book Clubs. And our Book Club is going to be the centerpiece of his study.

Book clubs are one of the biggest social groups in America … people want them … people need them. I know I do.

LILY. When you first brought it up, I thought it sounded like a hokey local cable access project. But, Ana, this is fantastic.

ROB. I've always secretly wanted to be on a reality show.

ANA. Rob. This is a serious documentary study by a renowned international director. Now as for the camera. *(Everyone looks at it.)* Look away! *(Everyone looks in different directions.)* Pretend it's not there. Act natural. Make yourselves comfortable. More comfortable. *(All pretending to be relaxed and comfortable … but not succeeding.)* It'd not be out of the realm of possibility that this could end up in Cannes.

WILL. Cannes! Fantastic!

JEN *(blurts)*. It's dreadful.

ANA. Excuse me?

JEN *(beat, touches her lips)*. I said that out loud, didn't I?

LILY & WILL. You did.

JEN. I'm really sorry. I didn't mean to …

WILL. Jenny, this is a great opportunity for our Book Club.

JEN. But why does our Book Club need an opportunity?

ANA. Because when a wonderful Book Club works so well for so long, it becomes our responsibility to share it with others.

JEN. But won't having THAT bug-eyed thing looking at us— change us?

ANA. Lars Knudsen is very clear—Nothing will change. We will take turns picking the books. All of us will read it and discuss. The big difference is we will meet here for filming every two weeks.

LILY. A new book every two weeks?!

ANA. Lars has some film festival deadlines; I thought we could handle the reading pressure.

WILL. Of course we can handle the reading! Right?

ALL. Right.

WILL. After all, Book Club is all about the books.

ROB. I thought Book Club was about the food.

ANA. Book Club is food for the mind and nourishment for the soul. And since I am the one that dragged us all into this crazy adventure, here at our house, I will be happy to cook all the meals

WILL. Glorious food by Ana.

LILY. But can we use your kitchen to cook when it's our book?

ANA. Use my kitchen?

JEN. Or just order take-out?

ANA. Take out? *(Beat.)* Of course! Whatever you need. Your book. Your meeting. It will just happen to be at our house.

LILY. With a freaky looking camera on us.

(All laugh.)

ANA. Rob, why don't you bring in the wine and lox dip I whipped up?

ROB. Great idea, Ana

ANA. And let us begin with Will's book selection *Moby Dick* or *The Whale* by Herman Melville. A classic American novel.

WILL. "Call me Ishmael. Some years ago—never mind how long precisely—having little or no money in my purse, and nothing particular to interest me on shore, I thought I would sail about a little and see the watery part of the world. Whenever I find myself growing grim about the mouth; whenever it is a damp drizzly November in my soul; whenever it requires strong moral principle to prevent me from deliberately stepping into the street or knocking people's hats off, then I account it high time to get to the sea as soon as possible. This is my substitute for pistol and ball."

ANA. Sublime reading, Will.

WILL. Thank you, Ana.

ROB. Great job, buddy.

LILY. A classic in every sense of the word. Right, Jen?

JEN *(madly reading a beat-up soft cover, looks up)*. I'm not finished yet.

LILY. OH! AS I WAS SAYING: I—

ANA. Lily, you know, we have a rule about turning off cell phones before Book Club.

WILL. Book Club is just like the theater.

LILY. Oh Ana, no worries. My Kindle is on the fritz and I left my iPad charging at work. I just downloaded *Moby Dick* for free onto my cell.

WILL. Really?

LILY. It's easy and in the public domain.

ANA. I just like the feel of a real book: the paper, the cover.

LILY. But this is the future. *(To the camera.)* And this saves trees!

ANA. Right. As I was about to say: we could focus the whole conversation on the first line alone! Who is "Ishmael"?

LILY. Did you know Ishmael is the Biblical name of a social outcast and—

ROB. Wait. All I needed was to read the first line?

WILL. But, Rob, if you only read the first line, then you wouldn't know what happens at the end.

JEN *(blurts)*. Finished!

ROB. Oh, I know what happens. In the end, poor Moby Dick dies.

JEN. Not really, Rob. *(Beat.)* The ending is still very fresh for me.

ROB. Moby doesn't die?

WILL. The White Whale can never die.

LILY. He is God

ANA. He is destiny.

JEN. He is nature.

ROB. Oh.

ANA. You didn't read the book, did you, Rob?

ROB. It's 615 pages dense and long … and I love animals.

ANA. Rob—

ROB. Seriously, I tried, Ana, I really tried.

ANA. Thank you for trying

LILY. Will, I wasn't surprised that *Moby Dick* was your book choice.

ANA. Why is that, Lily?

LILY. It's just such an ambitious … and male book. Captain Ahab seeking revenge on the whale that destroyed his leg.

WILL. Thank you, Lily. Funny, his book got terrible reviews when it first came out. And now it's a great American classic.

JEN. I suppose people just thought of it as a popular adventure book.

ROB. How could this be popular? It's so long.

JEN. I learned so much from this book … About life. About people. About harpoons …

WILL. My favorite line was, "Better to sleep with a sober cannibal than a drunken Christian."

LILY. Which makes me wonder if there's a homosexual subtext, between Queequeg the Cannibal and Ishmael.

WILL *(beat)*. I don't think so.

LILY. Queequeg has to be gay.

ANA. Queequeg is not gay.

WILL. Queequeg is a cannibal.

LILY. Maybe a bi-curious cannibal?

(LILY and JEN laugh.)

ANA. This is an American classic, Lily.

LILY. I know! And this American classic is filled with homoerotic subtext.

JEN. Is there subtext in the title?

(Everyone laughs varying degrees of laughter, less from ANA.)

ANA. That's so funny. But "Dick" meant something different back then. Perhaps, we should deepen instead of broaden, don't you think?

ROB. Well, isn't Moby Dick a SPERM whale?

(JEN snorts, she laughs so hard. This time, ANA is not amused.)

ANA. Jen, we are trying to have a serious conversation here.

JEN. Sorry. I'm working too much and sleeping too little.

LILY. No matter, this book is a long beautiful ode to "man love."

WILL. Really?

LILY. Page 113, "Some old couples often lie and chat over old times till nearly morning. Thus, then, lay I and Queequeg—a cosy, loving pair." Isn't that homoerotic?

WILL. No. That is just roommate stuff. Right, Rob?

ROB. Right.

WILL. Rob and I were roommates in college.

LILY. Oh, I wondered how you guys got to be friends.

WILL. Rob was the handsome, athletic type from a very good family.

ANA. His grandfather was a brilliant scientist that helped invent the birth control pill!

ROB. My middle name is "Novum."

ANA. Will, on the other hand, was more hard-working and organized.

WILL. I liked making thematic window displays in my parent's little grocery store. Corn, corn flakes. Corn syrup.

ANA. A born museum curator.

LILY. Well, it's cool that two such different men can be so close.

(WILL and ROB high-five)

ROB & WILL. Oh yeah!

LILY. It's refreshing to see a jock and a gay man as best friends.

(The men are about to bump elbows or high-five again and freeze. Stunned pause.)

ANA. Lily—Will is not gay.

LILY *(laughs)*. That's a good one! *(Laughs. Stops.)* Wait, you're serious?

JEN. Very serious.

LILY *(laughs a little)*. Really?

WILL. Lily, I am not gay.

(LILY absorbs the fact, the room.)

LILY. Oh Will, I'm sorry. *(Sees the camera.)* I am so sorry. I just—

ROB. Lily, why would you think Will is gay?

LILY. Ah … I don't … know … *(Looks around for help. JEN looks down at her hands.)*

WILL. Is it the way I dress?

LILY. No. That's—not—

ANA. I love the way you dress, Will.

LILY. It's very elegant.

WILL. Is it my voice?

LILY. Not at all!

ROB. You have a total guy voice, Will.

WILL. Or my love of literature—or musical theatre—?

LILY. Noooo!

ANA. Will, I'm sure Lily meant nothing of the sort.

LILY. Ana is right. And besides, everyone knows gay is cool. Very cool.

WILL. Not one of us is disparaging gayness in any form. I'm just curious what made you think I was gay.

LILY. Oh, I don't know what made me say that … Maybe it's because you are almost 40 years … young! And unmarried and I assumed …

WILL. Oh, so do you think Jen's gay too?

LILY. No!

WILL. So Jen's not cool enough to be gay?

LILY. That's not what I meant at all.

JEN. Hey! I'll have you know, I kissed a girl my sophomore year of college.

ROB & WILL *(look at LILY)*. Really?

LILY. Who didn't!

ROB & WILL. Really?

(ROB and WILL turn hopefully to hear the same thing from ANA.)

ANA. Lily, Will was my first real kiss.

LILY. Oh! Really?

WILL. Freshman year. We were each other's first real love.

ANA. Long walks by the river, picnics in the park,

WILL. We kissed under the elms.

ANA. We did.

WILL. Beautiful Ana was all mine, until this handsome bastard stole her away and broke my heart. Right, buddy?

ROB. Right.

ANA. Rob and I fell for one another during crew practice.

ROB. Ana was my coxswain.

ANA. Something about the way Rob rowed really … rocked my boat.

ROB. All I had to do was look at Ana's mouth … opening and closing, telling … me … what to do.

WILL. They tried to hide it from me. Until I walked in on them in the heat of lovemaking!

ANA. Oh God! I was mortified.

ROB. Will was so upset. He screamed at us, then threw a book at me.

WILL. *Paradise Lost* by Milton.

ROB. In hardback. It knocked me out.

WILL. And then I turned to run for help and broke my nose against the door.

ANA. Things were so intense and passionate between us back then. We all found each other at the hospital, hurt and bruised, and I wept for the pain I caused these two wonderful men ... whose friendship was torn apart because they both loved me. I vowed to myself that I would bring us back together by building something strong and beautiful which became our Book Club. And my men agreed.

WILL *(beat)*. I thought Book Club was my idea.

ANA. No, it was my idea.

WILL. Oh, because I thought—

ANA. Will, it was my idea that I shared with you, my book lover!

WILL *(flattered)*. Oh, Ana.

LILY. How inspiring! After all that heartbreak, you are all still friends.

JEN. It's a pretty amazing love story, huh?

ROB. Ana and I got married. Will was the best man.

WILL. At their ceremony, I read a gorgeous excerpt of *Paradise Lost*.

LILY. Who would have thought *Moby Dick* would bring out so much personal revelation?

ANA *(from the end of the book)*. "Towards thee I roll, thou all-destroying but un-conquering whale; to the last I grapple with thee; from hell's heart I stab at thee; for hate's sake I spit my last breath at thee, thou damned whale!"

(People clap.)

WILL. God, I love Book Club!

ANA. Now honey, don't you wish you had read the book?

ROB. Maybe if I got to pick something I liked.

WILL. Ana has been taking your turn for the past five years, Rob.

ANA. Oh honey, I'm sorry! I thought you liked it that way.

ROB. I did. But I think I would like to take my turn back now.

ANA. Oh Rob! Really? *(Hugs him.)*

WILL. What do you want to read, buddy?

ROB. Something fun and exciting.

JEN. Can I suggest a new rule that it be less than 400 pages?

ROB. Absolutely!

ANA. It will be a window into your soul, Rob.

LILY. Rob, just pick a book and we will all read it with you.

ROB. Right now? I don't know what to pick right now!

ANA. Listen, honey. Jen has already selected her book for the next meeting, right?

JEN. *The Age of Innocence* by Edith Wharton. An American classic set in 1870s New York. 278 pages.

LILY. Nice choice, Jen!

WILL. Rob, that gives you two weeks to choose your book. And then we will all read yours. OK?

ROB. OK! Jen, I promise I'll read your book too.

ANA. We'll see …

JEN. That would be great!

LILY. Good night everyone. Thank you. The dip was great.

ANA. Don't mention it.

LILY. Again, Will. I'm sorry for my assumption about you.

WILL. Worry not, dear Lily. As you know, you can't judge a book by its cover.

LILY. I'll say.

WILL. You of all people should know that!

(Beat. The whole room freezes.)

LILY. Oh—Why? Because I'm … from Akron, Ohio?

WILL. No. No. Yes! But … I love … Akron, Ohio.

LILY. Me too! Some of my best friends are "Akron-Americans."

WILL. Oh, Lily … I'm sorry. I just put my foot in my mouth.

LILY. Will, I did the exact same thing too. And I'm sorry as well. *(They hug.)* Good night, Will.

WILL. Good night, Lily!

JEN. Will, can I have a ride?

WILL. Did you lose your keys again?

JEN. They're not lost. They're just not with me.

WILL. C'mon then! Thanks for everything, everybody. Bye, Ana, my love.

JEN. Thanks! Bye everyone!

(Everyone dashes out. LILY looks at ANA and ROB.)

ANA. Lily, that hug between you and Will is what Book Club is all about.

LILY. I'm sorry, I just really thought Will was gay!

ANA. Lily, I didn't want to embarrass Will, but the discomfort you sense from him is because he is still in love with me.

LILY. Omigoodness.

ANA. Rob and I have discussed it …

ROB. We have.

ANA. And there's nothing we can do but try to make Will feel as happy and comfortable as we can.

LILY. It's a testament to your friendship that Book Club works as well as it does.

ANA. Oh Lily. I see so much of myself in you. You are a great writer … and you're already so connected to the pulse of this city! You are heading straight for the top!

LILY *(laughs)*. I don't know about that. But thank you for your help and support. Good night, Ana. Good night, Rob

ROB. Good night, Lily.

(LILY leaves.)

ROB *(cont'd)*. Well, that went well!

ANA. Oh, I really hope so …

ROB. Your dip was great.

ANA. Thanks … but … I just … *(She looks at the camera lowers her voice.)* Oh forget it.

ROB. Is it because of the camera?

ANA. I'm sure Lars will edit this out.

ROB. OK. Then.

ANA. I mean that "Sperm whale" joke, Rob? Was that necessary?

ROB. Jen laughed!

ANA. And Lily's assumption about Will. And Jen arriving late. And Will offending Lily! Rob, what are the Danes going to think about us when they see that?!

ROB. You said we should be ourselves.

ANA. I mean "our better selves."

ROB. Our better selves?

ANA. Book Club is about elevating our conversation, our thoughts, our souls through great literature. And being brave and trying new things and allowing the world to see how reading improves our lives. This documentary means a lot to me.

ROB. Is that why you told everybody, in front of the camera, that I was a disappointment?

ANA. What? When? I would never say that about you!

ROB. After I said I would read *The Age of Innocence*—You said: "We'll see … "

ANA. Rob, I love you, but why do you come to Book Club and never read the books!? You are missing the whole point!

ROB. I think the books are just an excuse to hang out, eat and be … people.

ANA. Yes, but the best people you can be!!! *(Beat.)* Sorry, honey. It's really *my* problem not yours. I just need to be a stronger me and make my peace with it.

ROB. Ana, you wait and see! I am going to read *The Age of Innocence* if it's the last thing I do.

(ROB storms off.

Lights shift.

Projection: **ELSA JONES-EISENBLITZ, Literary Agent, New York, N.Y.**

Spotlight on ELSA [played by PUNDIT or JEN]. She is wearing big eyeglasses, a shawl.)

ELSA. Humans need five things … four of which we share with other animals: water, food, shelter and sex. The unique fifth thing humans need is story. The sixth thing is stories about sex—hell, I'm kidding!

But, seriously, there are like seven billion people that inhabit our planet, and every one of us has a story. Some, like my father, keep their story inside; most, like my mother, tell theirs to the neighbors, and a few like, 2 billion people, take the time to jot something down for posterity.

Writing a book is hard work. It takes heart. It takes discipline; it even sometimes takes, God help me, talent.

I can't even tell you how many millions of manuscripts are submitted each year, but it's a friggin' heartbreaking colossal number. And these are the facts. Of the millions and millions of manuscripts that are submitted each year only 250,000 are published. And out of the 250,000 books that are published, most Americans read an average of less than three. You do the math.

Writing a book takes courage. Getting it published takes luck.

But getting someone to read your book takes a friggin' miracle.

(Lights out.

Projection: The Age of Innocence by Edith Wharton*.)*

ANA. Lars Knudsen has provided us with one or two talking points. Let me open the envelope.

WILL. Practice for the Oscars, maybe?

ANA. Ah-ha! "What book had the deepest impact on you, when you were young?"

(Ad-lib murmurs and responses.)

LILY. *Sounder* changed my childhood.

WILL. Oh, my God. *Sounder*!

LILY. Read it in fourth grade and I cried until snot plopped on the pages. Life for a poor share-cropper was hard enough, but did they have to kill his dog?

WILL. A brutal book.

JEN. That ending nearly killed me.

ANA. For me it was *Old Yeller*.

(Everybody moans their appreciation.)

LILY. It's wonderful how dead dogs bring the world together.

(Everyone laughs.)

ROB *(pause)*. When I was fifteen—

ANA. Honey, don't look at the camera.

ROB. When I was fifteen, I liked reading those books about the NFL … you know, they were this thin and they had a blurry picture of the player on it. My father was not happy. Junior, can't you read something serious? Something classic? Something British? Oh yeah, Dad?! How about *Tarzan of the Apes*?

After reading that book, something in me clicked. I volunteered at the local zoo and helped sweep the gorilla pavillion. You know what's amazing? Putting your hand up to the window and having a gorilla do the same thing. So human-like … I promised myself that when I grew up, I would move to Africa and work with baby gorillas.

JEN. I didn't know that.

ANA. Rob has a very big heart, you know.

ROB. Instead, I grew up, got married and went into pharmaceutical sales.

ANA. And he just got a fantastic promotion! Rob was offered a vice-president position in the company!

LILY. Wow, in this economy?

JEN. That's great!

ROB. We are a pharmaceutical company. Recession is great for depression. Will, what was your book?

WILL. *The Little House*. I remember the pictures very vividly. It was the true story of this cute little pink house that was in the middle of a field … and how the world encroached on it, and it became a little pink house shadowed by enormous skyscrapers and cowering beneath supersonic jets until … someone had the decency to scoop it up and put in a field where it could just be. It's a true story of the historical preservation society's heroic efforts to find a home for that house. And a clear indication of my early love for history.

JEN. I fell in love when I was fourteen. Hard. The kind of love that makes you jittery, that fills you with hope and despair all at once. I look for him in every guy I kiss: Heathcliff.

LILY. Heathcliff!

JEN. What an asshole! And I'll be damned if *Wuthering Heights* hasn't ruined me in some way.

ROB. I just don't get it.

JEN. Get what?

ROB. My company makes billions of dollars selling pills that make people feel less sad. And here you are, delighting in reading books that are full of heartbreak, despair and dead dogs.

LILY. You should read *Wuthering Heights*, Rob.

JEN. It breaks your heart in the best way.

ROB. Why not read something that makes us happy?

JEN. *Wuthering Heights* makes me happy. Nothing beats getting swept up like that … in the characters, in the story.

ANA. The beautiful lush language.

WILL. The breathless yearning.

LILY. And there's always the hope!!! The happy ending.

JEN. Exactly! That's the most painful part. That goddamn hope!!!

LILY. Hope is hell! And I love it!

WILL. Me too!

JEN. To hope! To hell! And to *Wuthering Heights*!

ROB. But you said *Wuthering Heights* kind of ruined you!!

WILL. I think Jen might be saying that her romantic notions have hurt her in the past.

JEN *(blurts)*. Ah, my scandal.

LILY. What scandal?

JEN. Can I have more wine, please?

ANA. Oh Jen, forget it! It happened so long ago … old news.

LILY. I'm sorry. I didn't mean to be nosey.

JEN. Oh God. Lily, I'm sorry. You are a part of our Book Club family. You should know.

ANA. Jen, no worries. Lily can Google it at home: alone.

JEN. But we are a community. Lily, remember some years ago the scandal involving a young legal intern and a certain married Senator.? The total implosion of the state senate? "The Mouse that Brought Down the House?"

LILY. Ohmigod! You were the mouse!

ANA. Jen … you really don't have to …

JEN. I left my job in disgrace; tax payers picketed the Senate, people were fired; his wife divorced him …

ANA. We try to never talk about it.

JEN. I lost everything. My heart. My job. My law school scholarship. And just when I thought there was no hope. I got a phone call from my old friend Will.

WILL. I said, "Jenny, get out of bed, and come to Book Club."

JEN. And I did. That phone call meant the world to me.

ANA. And we are so lucky to have Jen as a friend and Book Clubber. The end!

ROB. See? That's what I'm talking about! A happy ending!!

LILY. Jen, thank you for sharing.

JEN. Thank you.

WILL. Catharsis.

JEN. Now, Ana, if we could just stop and rewind the camera, before we go on.

ANA. Oh, Jen, no.

JEN. No?

ANA. Jen, That box it is in … it's locked. We can't touch the camera.

JEN. What?! I assumed, Ana, you would have control of it.

ANA. Me? Have control? Why would you think that?

JEN. Umm—I just—

ANA. Jen, didn't you read the release before you signed it?

JEN *(beat)*. Oh-my-God … Lars—Lars—edit out what I just said. Cut it! Please.

ANA. Jen—please don't talk to the camera.

WILL. Jenny, it's OK.

JEN. It's not. I was sharing with Lily. Not Lars! I can't … I don't want an audience in my life.

ANA *(gently)*. Audience? Do you see an audience?

(All look out at the audience.)

JEN. Guys, I don't think I want to be part of this film.

ANA *(pause)*. Jen, I love you and if you don't want to be a part of this film, I respect that.

JEN. Ana, thank you.

ANA. You will just have to find a time to meet up with us after Book Club.

JEN. What?

ANA. Or you can rejoin Book Club in three months after Lars' film is done.

ROB. What? No!

WILL. That's not what Ana means …

LILY. No Jen at Book Club?

WILL. Jenny, do you want to leave Book Club?

JEN. No. You know how much I love reading the books and how I look forward to discussing them with you. Ana, Book Club kind of saved my life.

ANA. I know, Jen. And it wouldn't be Book Club without you.

WILL. Book Club needs you!

ROB. Plus, I love your nachos and refried beans, Jen. *(Takes a bite.)*

JEN. You guys …

ANA. Nachos is such an original choice to complement a book like *The Age of Innocence*. What is your recipe for the refried beans?

JEN. You know … a can.

WILL. Please stay.

ROB. We need you. And your nachos.

ANA. You add crunch to our meetings.

LILY. And besides, *The Age of Innocence* is fantastic.

JEN *(sits)*. What the hell. I need to talk about this book.

LILY. I also loved the Scorsese movie. Michelle Pfeiffer and Daniel Day Lewis.

JEN. Me too!

ROB. Wait! There's a movie of this? … By Martin Scorsese?

WILL *(ROB tries to break in a couple of times during WILL's speech)*. OK, Rob, let me fill you in. The book takes place in New York, in the late eighteen hundreds. Newland Archer is the main character. He's a stuffy, class-oriented snob that is about to marry this pretty, little, bland thing called May Welland. And he thinks he is happy, until he meets May's cousin, the exciting and exotic Countess Ellen Olenska, who is creating scandal by divorcing her husband, and living her life on her own terms. Archer is madly attracted to Ellen, forcing him to question all that he believes to be sacred and true—

ROB. I know that.

WILL. Oh. You do?

ROB. I read the book.

JEN. You did?

ANA. All of it, honey?

ROB. Yes, honey, all of it.

ANA. Rob! I'm so proud of you.

LILY. I loved *The Age of Innocence*! All that repressed passion stuffed into one haunted husband. It's excruciatingly painful and beautiful.

ROB. I hated *The Age of Innocence*.

JEN. What? Why?

ROB. It … troubled me. I couldn't sleep.

WILL. Rob, why did it bother you?

ROB. After reading this, I don't know, I wanted to, you know, scream. Or break something. I don't know, I guess … Listen … Chapter 30.

(ROB opens the book.)

ROB *(cont'd)*. "Never, in all the years to come, would May surprise him by an unexpected mood, by a new idea, a weakness, a cruelty or an emotion.

His wife had spent her poetry and romance on their short courting: the function was exhausted because the need was past.

He laid down his book and stood up impatiently; and at once she raised her head."

(ANA decides to be MAY in what she feels is a delightful interpretation.)

ANA. "What's the matter?"

ROB. "'The room is stifling: I want a little air.'

The mere fact of not looking at May, the fact of seeing a whole world beyond his world, cleared his brain and made it easier to breathe."

ANA. "Newland! Do shut the window. You'll catch your death."

ROB *(fires back)*. "'Catch my death!' he echoed; and he felt like adding: 'But I've caught it already … *(Discovery.)* I am dead. I've been dead for months and months.'"

(WILL, JEN and LILY along the way realize this is not a game to ROB.)

ANA. "Are you ill?"

ROB. "Poor May!"

ANA. "Poor? Why poor?"

ROB. "Because I shall never be able to open a window without worrying you … And I shall never be happy unless I can open the windows!"

"He paused, a man who longs for a change, and is yet too weary to welcome it. Something he knew he had missed … The flower of life." *(Beat.)* The flower of life.

(ROB closes the book.)

ANA. Thoughts? Impressions? Questions?

(ROB slowly sinks to the floor as ANA is talking.)

WILL. Rob, buddy, are you OK?

ROB. I don't think so.

ANA. Does your stomach hurt?

ROB. No. *(Rubs his chest.)*

WILL. Rob, is it your chest?

ANA. Your chest!

ROB. It's my heart.

WILL. YOUR HEART!!!!

ANA. What are your symptoms, honey?

ROB. Like something is … cracking.

LILY. Could it be a signs of … a panic attack? Or cardiac arrest?

ROB *(calmly)*. No. It's definitely not a heart attack.

ANA. Then what is it?

LILY *(pulls out her phone)*. Wikipedia MD will tell us.

WILL. You need some herbal tea.

(WILL exits.)

ANA. I should call our doctor.

ROB. Ana, I don't need a doctor.

LILY. Your computer. My phone is almost out of juice.

(LILY exits.)

ANA. You'll need my password. Rob—hang in there honey. Jen, look after him, please. *(Exits.)*

ROB. That book freaked me out! I'm so confused.

JEN. There. There.

ROB. Where is my flower of life, Jen? Where is my flower of life?

JEN. Rob, it's there. You have it.

(ROB suddenly kisses JEN. With passion. It's a good sweet kiss for both of them.)

ROB. Oh my God.

JEN *(shocked)*. Oh my God.

ROB. That was so sweet.

JEN. It was, but Rob, it didn't happen.

ROB *(opens his eyes)*. I am so sorry, Jen.

JEN. It's OK, Rob.

ROB. I don't do things like that. Ever.

JEN. I know. Forget about it. This. It didn't happen.

ROB. You're right. It did not happen.

(Both JEN and ROB turn and see the camera and gasp.)

JEN & ROB *(simultaneously)*. Oh-my-God!!!

(ANA enters.)

ANA. How's the patient, Jen?

JEN. I don't know!

ANA. What's the matter?

JEN. Heartburn! Rob has beartburn, right?

ROB. Yeah. Yeah. That's it.

ANA. Everyone, mystery solved. Rob has heartburn!

(LILY enters.)

LILY. That was third on the list.

ANA. Of course! Those canned refried beans!

JEN. I'm sorry.

WILL. I have some Pepto in my briefcase. I need a spoon.

ANA. I'll get a spoon.

LILY. I'll find Alka-Seltzer.

ANA. Lily—it's in the bathroom.

(LILY, ANA and WILL exit. JEN and ROB are alone. They agitatedly gesture to camera.)

ROB. Lars, listen! It was nothing!

JEN. Please! Cut! Cut! Cut!

ROB. Lars, for the love of God!!!!

(LILY enters, as do WILL and ANA. ROB and JEN stop.).

LILY. Alka-Seltzer

WILL. Pepto Bismol.

ANA. And an appropriately sized spoon.

WILL. This will make you feel so much better.

ANA. Pick your poison, honey.

(ROB opens wide. A spoonful of Pepto then a swig of Alka-Seltzer.)

ROB. I think I'm just going to lie here.

LILY. Do we need to cancel the rest of Book Club?

JEN. I think so. Yes!

ANA. Over heartburn? No!

WILL. After all that excitement I don't know if everyone is up
for spending the night talking about wannabe lovers.

(ROB moans and lies down.)

JEN. Agreed.

ANA. Honey, Lars Knudsen needs footage. We can't let him
down.

ROB. I don't want to let anybody down.

WILL. There is Cannes.

LILY. Well if we don't want to end early … did Lars send any
more of those "talking points in an envelope"?

ANA. Great idea! There is one addressed to you, Lily.

LILY. To me?

LILY *(opens it)*. "Lily Louise Jackson, as the newest member
in the Book Club. When and why did you join?" I was
invited to join the Book Club … what, three months ago?

ANA. Yes, about then.

LILY. It was such a nice surprise. Moving to a new city is
hard. I thought it might be nice to make some new friends
beyond Facebook.

JEN. Lily, you were an inspired choice. I mean, Ana described
you and brought your resume.

ANA. Lily Louise Jackson. A Summa Cum Laude from
Kenyon College.

WILL. And we voted to give you a trial run, no hesitation.

LILY. Oh, you voted on me?

ANA. Yes, we have a vetting process, you know.

LILY. I did not know that.

WILL. Well, we do.

LILY. Like affirmative action for Book Clubs?

(ROB sits straight up.)

LILY *(cont'd, laughs)*. GOTTCHA! I'm just kidding!

(ANA, JEN, WILL and ROB all laugh.)

ANA. See?! Fresh! Irreverent. Keeping us on our toes. You passed with flying colors. Everyone loved you.

JEN. That's the night we read *Black Like Me*.

LILY. Which I found interesting.

WILL. Me too.

ANA. Yes, we like to read very diverse things. International writers. Writers of color.

LILY. *Black Like Me* was written by a white man.

ANA *(beat)*. Yes it was. But I've read *Love in the Time of Cholera* by Gabriel García Márquez.

WILL. *Native Son* by Richard Wright.

JEN. *The Color Purple* by Alice Walker, *Beloved* by Toni Morrison and *Devil in a Blue Dress* by … what's his name …

LILY. Walter Mosely. You read all of those in Book Club?

JEN. No—

(JEN and WILL look at each other worried.)

WILL. Not in Book Club.

(Pause.)

ANA. Omigoodness. Please don't tell me we have only read dead white men in Book Club?

JEN. Edith Wharton is a dead white woman.

WILL. And we've read some white men that are alive.

ANA. Oh no! See Lily, this is why we need you, to keep us real.

WILL. It's a terrible oversight.

JEN. We must do … something!

LILY. Ladies, and gentlemen, calm down.

ANA. We just have to remedy the situation, immediately. We should just skip ahead and let Lily pick the book for next meeting.

ROB. But I was going to pick the next book. *Return of Tarzan*!

ANA. Rob, sweetheart, no! This Book Club is about respect, tolerance, and what's truly important: It's about real literature. Don't you think we should do the right thing and let Lily pick next?

ROB. Let's do the right thing. *(Lies back down.)*

(Beat.)

JEN. So Lily, the Book Club choice is yours.

ANA. Lily—Shake us up! Challenge us! Don't be scared to bring in literature that's provocative with a lot of "soul."

LILY. Really? Oh! OK! Provocative? With "soul"? *(Beat.)* How about *Twilight*?

ANA. *Twilight*?

WILL. *Twilight*??

JEN. Yeah! *Twilight*!

LILY. You know the bestseller about vampires?

ANA. Vampires …

LILY. I bet *Twilight* is full of "soul." Undead ones. *(She makes vampire gesture.)*

ANA *(uncomfortable beat)*. Fabulous

(Lights change.

Projection: FRANK, Secret Service Agent, Washington, D.C.

FRANK can be played by WILL or PUNDIT in dark glasses.)

FRANK. Book Clubs? Yeah, I know about Book Clubs. I've been in a Secret Service Book Club for fifteen years.

My favorite books are *A Farewell to Arms*, *The Old Man and the Sea* and *For Whom the Bell Tolls*, all by Ernest Hemingway.

The most important part of my life is Book Club. People come and go, but the Book Club stays. There are certain unalterable rules you must follow if you want Book Club to survive and thrive.

One: Trust no one. Everyone must be vetted by the Book Club. Sure so-and-so might be someone's best friend, but that doesn't mean he won't pose a serious threat to Book Club.

Two: Take no prisoners. If a rogue element does somehow infiltrate Book Club, you must be ruthless, absolutely ruthless, in removing him.

Three: Protect your leader. Book Club will collapse without the firm hand of authority and rule of law.

Ignore these rules at your Book Club's peril.

You have been warned.

(Projection: **Twilight by Stephenie Meyer**.

Lights on the Book Club: LILY, ROB, ANA, JEN and WILL.)

ANA. Before we talk about *Twilight*. I want to share something very important. Being with all of you has given me the opportunity to make a big change in my life.

ROB. What kind of change?

ANA. I have decided to take a leave of absence from my column.

ROB. Honey, you're telling me this now? With everyone? In front of the camera?

ANA. Rob, I thought you would be delighted by the surprise. You have that new promotion and raise! Besides it's just a short leave of absence. This documentary has made me realize I work too much at the paper. I need to make room for other life things.

ROB. Oh honey! *(Kisses her.)* Let's have a baby! A sweet baby that is as smart and pretty as you!

JEN. So you two are thinking about a baby!!!?

ROB & ANA *(simultaneously)*. Yes! / No.

ROB. I thought you said you really wanted a baby.

ANA. I do but I'm taking a creative leave. I need to explore new things.

ROB. A baby is very new.

ANA. Honey, right now is not the right time.

ROB. Ana, we are not getting any younger …

ANA. Rob, I don't think this is the place … *(Refers to the camera.)*

ROB. Oh, I thought this was the perfect place to make huge personal life decisions!

ANA. Rob, can I talk to you over here? Off camera? Everyone, carry on.

(ROB follows ANA "off camera." Everyone sits awkwardly. The focus is on the Book Club listening to the private conversation off camera. They can hear everything.)

ANA *(offstage)*. Rob, what is wrong with you?

ROB *(offstage)*. I want a baby. I want to take care of something … smaller … and bigger than just us. I want the flower of life.

ANA *(offstage)*. Rob, we are in the middle of Book Club.

ROB *(offstage)*. Are we going to have a baby or not?

ANA *(offstage)*. Of course … just not right this second.

ROB *(offstage)*. I don't think you want one.

ANA *(offstage)*. I love babies! LOVE THEM. Ask anyone. *(Comes back into the room with ROB.)* Jen, Will, Lily. Don't I love babies?

WILL. Doesn't everybody?

ROB. Loving babies and wanting to have one are two different things.

LILY. You know, kids aren't for everyone.

WILL. That's what I tell my staff every time they want to create a touch-and-feel vase exhibit for children.

JEN *(blurts)*. I really want to have a baby. *(Covers her mouth.)*

LILY. Wow, Jen.

  (Beat.)

ANA. Oh Jen! Are you dating someone again?

JEN. No. I'm not. And time is ticking … and here I am: dreaming of being a mom …

WILL. You would be a terrific mom!

JEN. I know. But I haven't found my Heathcliff!

LILY. Have you thought of a sperm bank?

JEN. A sperm bank? Oh. No. It sounds too sterile and impersonal.

LILY. My cousin used one! I helped her read through all the potential dad profiles. It was like sperm-bank speed dating. And now she has a beautiful baby boy.

JEN. I've always imagined my life with children.

ROB. I love horsing around with my nieces and nephews!

WILL. Jenny, you would be a wonderful mother.

JEN. Thank you, guys.

ANA. I am in awe. Of course Jen would be … very loving. It's just it is so much work. Good mothers are organized, and firm, and consistent.

JEN. I think lots of good mom's embrace the chaos of kids. Kids need love more than anything.

ROB. I would LOVE to be a stay at home dad.

ANA. Rob, I'm not against having children, just not right now. Jen, I am so proud of you but I am so concerned; what would you do when you are alone, and the kid is crying and you can't find your keys? How will you cope? Prozac helps with your depression, but it won't change your baby's diapers.

(All are suddenly deeply aware of the camera. Pause.)

ANA *(cont'd)*. I'm so sorry.

ROB. We should talk about this later, Ana. You know, without an audience.

WILL. I think it would be great to get to the book. Now.

LILY *(holds up her Kindle)*. *Twilight* by Stephenie Meyer!

(The doorbell rings.)

WILL. The doorbell!

ANA. Who could that be, at this time?

JEN. No! Oh no! I can't believe it. He showed up.

LILY. Who showed up?

JEN. Alex. This guy in my building. We were in the laundry room in the basement and he … he was reading *Twilight*!

(Pause.)

WILL. Jenny—you know—that's not the way we do things.

JEN. I'm sorry. He was reading the book and he looked so sad. I blurted out the invitation and then I just couldn't take it back.

ANA. Oh, Jen.

WILL. Jenny, he could be an axe murderer for all we know.

LILY. He can't be all bad. He was reading the book selection.

WILL. That's exactly why I am concerned.

LILY. Is he cute?

JEN. He's not my type, but he's interesting. He had a lot of smart things to say about … vampires.

ANA. Oh no.

JEN. The poor guy just broke up with his girlfriend.

LILY. Oh, no.

(Doorbell rings again.)

JEN. I need to open that door.

ANA & WILL. WAIT!

JEN. I just invited him. On an impulse. That's all.

WILL. He has not been vetted by the group and it is just inappropriate to put us in this position.

ANA. Jen, he's going to have to come back another day.

LILY. That's silly, if he's read the book.

ROB. What does it matter if he has read the book!?

(Doorbell rings.)

JEN. I thought you would like him.

LILY. Oh this is ridiculous. There are five of us and only one of him. What harm can this man do?

ANA. Lily, you are right!

(Light on ALEX. He enters.)

ALEX. Book Club, I presume?

ANA. Everyone, this is Jen's friend, Alex.

ALEX. We are laundry mates. Hi, Jen.

JEN. Hi, Alex.

ANA. I'm Ana Smith. Welcome to my home and my Book Club.

WILL. Our Book Club.

ALEX. So this is the Book Club? It's not what I expected. At all.

LILY *(laughs and goes to shake his hand)*. Hello, Alex. I'm Lily.

ALEX. Hello, Lily

LILY. And this is Rob, Ana's husband. And this is Will.

ALEX. Hey.

ROB. Hey.

WILL. Hello.

ALEX. Hello, Book Club.

ANA. Thank you Lily, for the introductions.

ALEX. So no one here is a vampire?

ANA. God, no!

ALEX. There's always someone in a group wanting to suck the life out of someone.

(LILY laughs. ALEX notices the camera.)

ALEX. Whoa what's that?

JEN. Oh that's the bug-eyed camera I was telling you about.

ANA. Our Book Club is the subject of a Lars Knudsen documentary.

ALEX. Lars Knudsen! Impressive. *(Waves.)* Hi, Lars!

WILL. Please do not look at the camera!

ALEX *(looks at the audience)*. Oh. *(Shuns his face.)* OK.

ANA. Just try to forget it's there.

LILY. Please have a seat, Alex.

ALEX. How about *Twilight*? Did *Twilight* make you tingle all over?

LILY. It certainly stirred some feelings …

ANA. Excuse me?

WILL. Is that an appropriate question to ask on a first … Book Club?

JEN. Lily, it totally made me tingle, too!

ROB. Really?

ANA. Rob didn't read the book!

WILL. Lucky Rob.

LILY. OK, let me fill you in. A young seventeen-year-old girl, Bella Swan, moves to the rainy town of Forks in the state of Washington to live with her father. She describes herself as clumsy and ordinary.

ALEX. But all the boys in school, even the elusive, hyper-handsome Edward Cullen, seem interested in her.

LILY. That's right!

ALEX. Edward is attracted to Bella because the scent of her blood beckons him.

LILY. You see: Edward Cullen is a vampire.

WILL. A vegetarian vampire—

ROB. So that's why we had tofu for dinner.

WILL. And he hungers for Bella—to go to prom with him.

ROB. Prom? How can a vampire go to high school?

WILL. He's been seventeen for a hundred years.

ROB. But doesn't the sun kill vampires?

LILY. No, the sun makes Edward sparkle.

ALEX. Like glitter.

ROB. You're making this up.

JEN. Actually the author, Stephenie Meyer, made it up.

ALEX. Apparently, not all vampire cultures are the same.

ANA. There is NOTHING cultured about this book.

WILL. Amen.

LILY. Edward loves Bella but also yearns to drink her blood. And she loves him. But they can't make love …

ALEX. Because he's scared that in the heat of passion, he would lose control and … eat her.

(LILY looks down at her Kindle and perhaps reads a passage from the book. Maybe the three things of which Bella is certain. JEN sighs loudly in response to the passage.)

WILL. Well, I'll just say this. I thought this book was dreadful. No action, poorly written. It's sexist and stupid. The heroine is a love-sick girl willing to give everything up for a vampire boy.

ANA *(agreeing with WILL)*. Just look at how Edward is described in chapter thirteen.

(Perhaps ANA reads aloud the passage where Bella admires Edward while lying in the meadow. Perhaps JEN, LILY and ROB sigh in response to the passage.)

WILL. Ana, I highlighted the same ridiculous paragraph!

ANA. This is certainly not literature.

ALEX. Oh, and what makes something literature?

ANA. Not vampires! Not poor writing. Not poor plot. This is trivial!

LILY. Since when is the pursuit of love trivial, Ana?

ALEX. Your point about *Twilight* not being literature is interesting, Annie.

ANA. It's not Annie. It's not Anna. It's Ah-nuh.

ALEX. Ah-nuh, gotcha. I know oodles about books. I am a professor of comparative literature.

ROB. You are a professor?

ALEX. Up for tenure this year. And guess what? The woman of my dreams dumped me at the altar. It was very dramatic. You want to know why she dumped me?

ANA, LILY, ROB, JEN & WILL. Why?

ALEX. Because of a book: "Alex," she said, "You are NOTHING LIKE EDWARD CULLEN." And I said "Edward … who?" And she said, "That's exactly your problem. You have lost your passion. You have no clue."

JEN. Oh, I'm sorry.

ALEX. And she was right. I have lost my passion. I have no clue! I am completely out of touch. *Twilight* is a phenomenon. It has sold over 100 million copies and been translated into thirty-seven languages and yet, what did I know about Bella Swan and Edward Cullen? Nothing!!! Have you heard of *Fifty Shades of Grey*—???

JEN & LILY *(look at each other)*. Maybe …

ALEX. Well, that bestseller was inspired from *Twilight* fan fiction. And yet what do I know about inner goddesses and sadomasochist sex contracts? Apparently, not enough! And what's District 12 and who's Katniss and why play a *Hunger Game*? More than 350 million *Harry Potter* books have been sold worldwide, and what can I tell you about Hogwarts? Squat! I've never cracked open a Mary Higgins Clark, a John Grisham or a Tom Clancy paperback. Never.

LILY. Really?

ALEX. And I am a professor of comparative literature!

LILY. Did you know romance is the most popular genre in modern literature? That Harlequin sells around four books a second!

ALEX. I am willfully oblivious to so much.

WILL. In this case, I would say willful oblivion is a very smart choice.

ANA. Just because millions of people like these books doesn't mean they're good. Popularity is not quality.

LILY. So you think ignoring what millions of people read or think is better?

WILL. This is a free country. If I read *Ulysses* instead of *Harry Potter* … that is my choice.

ANA. You have not read *Ulysses*, Will.

WILL *(icy)*. But I could!

JEN. Well, I've read all seven of the *Harry Potter* books.

LILY. Me too.

ROB. I love the *Harry Potter* movies.

ANA. I am proud to say I have not succumbed at all.

ALEX. And that is precisely my problem. What I think I am trying to say … is that a cultured person … a truly cultured person is connected—to the culture around him. A truly cultured person is … curious. You don't have to always like it … but you should try to experience it.

ANA. Popular culture is about entertainment. I am talking about enlightenment.

ALEX. A truly cultured person reads Salman Rushdie and Danielle Steel. A truly cultured person sees *La Traviatta*, *Swan Lake* and *American Idol*; a truly cultured person listens to Bach and Beyoncé!!!!

LILY. It's terrible. I've never been to the opera.

JEN. Me neither.

ALEX. I have the best job in the world. My work is to read and talk about books all day! But reading stopped giving me any pleasure. How horrible is that? I lost my curiosity. I lost my connection. Now, I want that feeling … back! And how do I do that??

ROB. Tell me: how?

ALEX. I'll tell you how: *Twilight*.

ROB. Really? *(Picks up the book and starts to read it.)*

ANA. You cannot be serious! *Twilight* is not literature any more than ketchup is a vegetable.

ALEX. *Twilight* is the reason my girlfriend dumped me at the altar. And now I understand why. *Twilight* touched something primal in her; it made her want to feel passion, mystery and experience love that is worth undying for.

WILL. See? It's a terrible harmful book.

ALEX. Today, on campus, one of my students, Ming Woo, a very shy girl, who never speaks in class, interrupted my *Twilight* reading to tell me how much she loved the entire series. She told me that she was a TWI-HARD, which is code for a die-hard *Twilight* fan and she was TEAM JACOB.

LILY. Team Jacob! Yeah!

JEN. I'm Team Edward all the way.

(LILY and JEN do a momentary mock vampire/werewolf hiss.)

ALEX. Suddenly, I had a common language, a connection, with this quiet teenaged kid I never had before. And as she delved into the virtues of Jacob the werewolf vs. Edward Cullen the vampire, it hit me: My God, maybe Edward Cullen is this century's version of Heathcliff!

LILY & JEN. HEATHCLIFF!!!

ANA & WILL. NO!!!

ALEX. We can debate all night on whether *Twilight* is good or bad … but *Twilight* is an important book.

ANA. Forgive me, Alex, for being a culture snob, but a few of us have to make sure there are standards. I for one don't want future generations to walk through the Museum of American Antiquities and think that the full essence of who we were as a people is McDonalds happy meals, *American Idol* and *Twilight*.

WILL. God, no.

ALEX. You know, Ana, I swore never to be part of a silly Book Club like this one! But this is great! This silly Book Club will be the very thing that reminds me of why I fell in love with books in the first place. Because right now, I don't love books, I don't love reading, and I think … I don't love anything anymore …

(Silence. JEN's cellphone goes off with a very hip, popular tune like something by Lady Gaga or Carly Jae Jepsen.)

JEN. My phone! Oh God, sorry! *(She turns it off.)*

ALEX. Sorry. I haven't been quite myself.

LILY. Wow, Alex, I'm glad you came. That's an amazing story.

ALEX. Thank you, Lily. *(Downs the wine.)* I'm glad I came too. A thousand pardons. I hope I didn't ruin the evening. Jen, thank you so much for inviting me. All of you, thank you for having me. Ana, your house is … perfect. Lily, thank you for selecting the book. *Twilight* feels like destiny. *(Another connection with LILY.)* I should go.

ANA. Yes, perhaps you should.

ALEX. Goodbye.

WILL. Goodbye.

JEN. Goodbye, Alex.

LILY. It was nice meeting you, Alex.

ALEX. Just out of curiosity. What is your next book?

ANA. I really think Will had a terrific idea and that *Ulysses* by James Joyce would be the perfect book for us. Don't you?

(Long pause.)

JEN. It's kind of long, isn't it? Like 900 pages.

LILY. I thought the book had to be 400 pages or less.

ROB. Is there a movie?

ANA. My friends, *Ulysses* is a masterpiece. It is ranked first on the list of 100 best novels of the 20th century.

WILL. I know we should read *Ulysses*, but is two weeks is enough time?

ALEX. Oh! Well if you are looking for a book that is under 400 pages, you can read in two weeks … and has lots of history …

WILL. History?

LILY. Yes?

ALEX. Why don't you read that old bestseller by Dan Brown: *The Da Vinci Code*? I hear it's fast and fun!

WILL. *The Da Vinci Code*?

ALEX. Have you read it, Will?

WILL. No, I have not.

ALEX. Me neither! But it's supposedly the most "popular book in the world." You should read that!

LILY. That's a great idea, Alex.

JEN. I already have it on my bookshelf.

ANA. Thank you for your input, Alex. But you are not a member of my Book Club—

WILL *(under his breath)*. Our Book Club—

ANA. And we've already selected *Ulysses*.

LILY. But Ana—it's not your turn. It's Rob's turn.

ROB. And I don't want to read *Ulysses*.

ANA. It's an amazing piece of work.

ROB. It's just not the right time, Ana.

JEN. How about *The Da Vinci Code*, Rob?

ROB. I don't know what I want!!

ANA. Of course you don't.

LILY. Well, I would like to read *The Da Vinci Code*.

JEN. Me too.

WILL. Well, I suppose it can't hurt; we only have two weeks. And the rule is 400 pages or less.

ANA. Fine! If that is what the Book Club wants then we will read *The Da Vinci Code*.

ALEX. I should go. I promise I will be much better behaved next time.

LILY. Great.

WILL. What—wait!!

ROB. Next time?

ANA. No—Alex, wait—you should know—

LILY. That we really look forward to seeing you here in two weeks!!!

JEN. Yes, we do.

(ANA is shocked speechless.)

ALEX. I'll be back with bells on! Thank you. I'm now reading *Search for Love* by Nora Roberts ... It's quite the page-turner.

(ALEX exits. LILY and JEN are giddy. WILL and ANA are horrified.)

JEN. Omigod.

LILY. Oh-my-God!

WILL. Oh—MY—GAWD!

ANA. That was … just … just … *(Shivers.)*

JEN. Ana, you look so pale.

ROB. Like a vampire.

ANA. What just happened?

WILL. That man … I just don't know what to say.

JEN. Wow.

ROB. What's WOW about that guy?

LILY. I thought Alex was great. I honestly thought this was our best Book Club ever.

WILL. You can't be serious.

JEN. He's smart.

LILY. And he's cute.

ROB. I thought he was weird.

ANA. But Lily, You must admit, he was a little out there. A little intense.

LILY. Isn't that the point?

ANA. Of course, of course, but intense in a … comfortable way.

JEN. Comfortably intense?

WILL. Fine, I'll say it! Alex was annoying.

ANA. So annoying.

LILY. I thought he was interesting.

ANA. That's interesting, because I found him intensely annoying!

JEN *(blurts without regret)*. But isn't intensely annoying a prerequisite for Book Club?

(Oops. All heads snap to JEN. Pause. Everyone looks at the camera.)

ANA. You know, we should just stop this conversation before any of us say anything we regret. If there's one thing of which I am certain it is that THAT man does not belong in our Book Club.

WILL. Any man that has so little regard for books should not come to Book Club.

LILY. He's a comparative lit professor.

WILL. Which shows a self-loathing that I think is beyond comprehension.

ANA. People, there is no need to discuss this, because he's not coming back.

JEN. I thought Alex was great!

ANA. I'm surprised we feel so differently about this.

JEN. I am too.

(Pause.)

LILY. Well, isn't there a vote?

WILL. Now you want rules?!

LILY. What's the big deal?

WILL. The big deal is respect!

JEN. You know, if Will feels this strongly about it, we should just … forget it.

LILY. You're right, Jen.

(Beat.)

WILL. Oh, so now I'm Dictator Will: intolerant, inflexible.

ANA. Nobody said that.

LILY. But Will, if we don't vote …

WILL. That's not the kind of man I am! Let us vote!

(ALEX bursts in.)

ALEX. Hello again.

(Everyone is startled.)

ALEX *(cont'd)*. Sorry, didn't mean to surprise you. I forgot my book.

(Silence.)

ALEX *(cont'd)*. I'm sorry. Did I interrupt something?

(All break into conversation kind of simultaneously overlapping.)

LILY. Yes.

ANA. No.

JEN. Just wrapping up …

WILL. Talking about the weather.

ROB. The book.

ALEX *(beat)*. You were all talking about me, weren't you?

LILY *(long pause)*. Well, yes, Alex, actually, we were talking about you.

ANA. We were just discussing whether you would fit into Book Club.

JEN. I'm sorry, Alex. I didn't know this would be so uncomfortable.

ALEX. Don't be sorry, Jen. And I would very much like to join Book Club, Ana.

LILY. He wants in.

ALEX. Yes, I do!

ANA. Ever since I started this Book Club—

WILL. We started this Book Club—

ANA. We have had a vetting process followed by a group vote.

ALEX. And?

LILY. We were about to vote before you walked in.

ALEX. Ah, a jury of my peers. May I watch?

WILL. This is a private affair. I don't think that's necessary.

ALEX. Private? But there's a camera!

WILL. Shh! Don't look at it! We are supposed to be acting completely unaware.

ROB. Like gorillas in the mist.

ALEX *(beat)*. Democracy is about transparency, isn't it?

(Pause.)

LILY. Well, for me, if there's a vote. I vote YES for Alex.

WILL *(beat)*. I love you, Lily, but I must vote my heart. I vote NO.

JEN. I vote yes.

(Beat.)

ANA. Jen, don't you love Book Club?

JEN. I think I love Book Club more than you do, Ana. And I think Alex will be good for us.

ANA. I love this Book Club more than you can imagine. No! I vote NO.

ALEX. That's two to two.

(Everybody slowly turns to ROB. Beat.)

ROB. Oh Shit!

(Lights out.

A **pause symbol** *is **projected on the screen**.)*

END OF ACT I

ACT II

(The **pause symbol** *is still on the screen. The* **play symbol** **replaces it.**

Projection: **SAM W. THOMPSON, Stock Manager for Wal-Mart, Amarillo, Texas**.

Spotlight on PUNDIT or ROB wearing a blue Wal-Mart vest with a nametag and smiley-face button.)

SAM. I can say without doubt that Book Clubs are truly an economic phenomenon and Wal-Mart is a proud participant, feeding the nation's hunger for books. Our pricing policies enable most families to be able to own and enjoy novels, biographies and bestsellers. And the numbers speak for themselves: over a million copies sold of *The Da Vinci Code*; *Harry Potter*, can't keep him on the shelf. *The Chicken Soup* books, sell like hot cakes.

And you know, not only do we encourage America to read, we encourage our employees by offering them a significant employee discount. I do believe we might have some intra-Wal-Mart Book Clubs, where employees from all Wal-Marts in a twenty-five-mile radius get together to discuss novels. And let me say something that I have no way of qualifying, but I believe that employees find these Book Clubs so satisfying that it has made the issue of unions completely irrelevant in our organization. *(Beat.)*

My favorite book? A personal question, no sure, I'm happy to address that … Just remember … not to judge a book by its cover. My favorite book … I would have to say is: well, I'll say it: *Lolita* by Vladimir Nabokov. Why? His use of language, humor, his ability to take the most horrid of situations and find a voice of humanity. Each turn of the phrase lands you in an unexpectedly original yet real place. *(Pause.)*

No, I'm afraid Wal-Mart does not carry *Lolita*.

(Projection: **The Da Vinci Code by Dan Brown**.*)*

LILY. Five-four-three-two-and it's seven p.m.!

ALEX. Hello, America. *(To the camera.)* Hello, Copenhagen!

ANA. You are ruining Lars Knudsen's fine film. You are ruining our Book Club.

ALEX. We just got started.

ROB. Alex, she's talking to me.

JEN. We agreed to let Alex join us just one more time, and see what happened.

ROB. I didn't vote. I didn't break the tie. I thought we should try to work it out,

ANA. Argh! We should have made it unanimous rule.

LILY. I think Rob's non-vote forced us to come up with a good compromise.

ANA. A one-time compromise.

LILY. So are we going to be adults about this? Or—

ANA. I'm so upset. I haven't been able to sleep.

ROB. Is there any food tonight?

ANA. Your "non-vote." His non-book. My non-food.

ALEX. Um yeah … well … I can order pizza.

ROB. I love pizza.

ALEX. And I have some *(Looks in his pocket.)* gum for everyone while we wait.

ALEX. So? How about *The Da Vinci Code* by Dan Brown.

ANA. Oh God, help me.

(ALEX opens the book.)

ALEX. Let's just start at the beginning. We meet the curator in the grand gallery and also the attacker.

(Perhaps ALEX reads a bit from the introduction of the curator and gallery. Also perhaps the bit describing the attacker.)

WILL. An albino!

ANA. Or the Easter Bunny—

ALEX. So what did you think of the book?

(Beat.)

LILY. Alex … I am so happy that you are here and I really really wanted to like this book …

ALEX. But …

LILY. It's very … plot driven, isn't it?

JEN. And the characters … well … they aren't real people, are they?

ANA. The language is flat and lifeless. It felt like I was reading two-dimensional movie. Not a real book.

ROB. Good because I saw the movie instead.

ANA. This is Book Club, Rob!

ROB. I like Tom Hanks. And it's the same story isn't it? And instead of investing twenty hours, I just used two. And you said so yourself, the book felt like a movie.

ANA. A movie is never better than a book.

ALEX *(to the camera)*. Lars, what do you think about that?

(ANA looks at the camera and annoyed at ALEX.)

ANA. What I mean is film cannot capture a whole book. Even if a book is—

WILL. I LOVED IT!!

ANA. Will?

WILL. I loved *The Da Vinci Code*. I loved every gasp-inducing, page-turning second in this book. I loved it so much I read it twice. I loved it so much, I want to go on a tour and see all the historic sites he talked about.

ANA. Will, are you all right?

WILL. Alex, this book. If I had read this book … ten years ago.

ANA. A lot of books have history in them, Will.

WILL. It's not just the history. It's not just the artifacts … although they are magnificent … but it's something more than that.

ROB. What?

WILL. There are secrets everywhere. The truth … is out there … hidden in plain sight.

JEN. Will, do you really think there are conspiracies?

WILL. Don't you?

JEN. I think conspiracies require a lot of organization and I don't see how—

WILL. Jenny, some of us thrive on organization. Some of us have everything tucked away exactly the way we think it should be. And yet, everyone is keeping secrets.

LILY. Isn't that a little paranoid, Will?

ALEX. Well, someone IS watching us …

(Everyone looks at the camera.)

WILL. Exactly. I mean that camera … do we really know Lars Knudsen is who he says he is?

ANA. He's a famous director!

WILL *(to the camera)*. Lars Knudsen, who are you, really?

ANA. Will, please stop talking to the camera.

LILY. Will is right. Is anyone who they say they are?

ANA. Of course. I am Ana Smith!

WILL. But weren't you Annie Gomez Krapowsky before you married Rob? Huh? Huh?

ALEX. You were an Annie.

ANA. That's hardly a secret.

WILL. All of us keep secrets … from each other. From ourselves. What are those secrets? What are your secrets?

(Beat. WILL looks around at each person. ANA looks for lint on her blouse, LILY checks her phone, ROB and JEN look at each other and away.)

WILL *(cont'd)*. Look at page five. The curator realizes that if he dies no one would know the truth and that horrifies him. He needs to pass on the secret, needs to find a way …

(Perhaps WILL reads the segment about the importance of the truth aloud.

Suddenly, WILL kisses ROB.

ANA, LILY & JEN. Will!

ANA. Oh MY God!

JEN. Oh my God.

ANA, LILY & JEN. Oh my GOD!

ROB. Will, buddy—

WILL. Rob, you are the only reason I want to come to Book Club.

ANA. He is the only reason?!

WILL. And the books. But I cannot live a lie any longer. I want you to know, Rob.

My secret is that I LOVE YOU.

(Shocked silence.)

ALEX. Rob, how do you feel about what Will just said?

ROB. Will. Thanks, but.

WILL. I know it's impossible. You don't need to love me back. But I want you to know: Rob, I've secretly loved you since freshman year.

ANA. That can't be true!

WILL. Alas, Ana it is. I'm in love with you, Rob … because you are you… and because I am … I am …

ANA. Will—

LILY. Oh my GOD! Will, you are gay!

WILL. I am? *(Beat. He looks at JEN.)*

JEN. Willy, I think maybe so …

WILL. I am? *(Pause.)* Oh my … Oh my … Oh my. *(He sits stunned.)* I think I might be gay.

ANA. Will, I know how private and discreet you are and just because you are under some pressure … I just don't want you to regret anything … or commit to something that isn't really true. Will, your parents may see this documentary one day.

WILL. Mom and Pop?

ANA. Yes … working in their little grocery store … think of them

WILL. Hey, Mom and Pop. Guess what? *(Stands up.)* I'm GAY! I'm GAY!

(He stops and starts to cry with relief.)

ROB. Hey, buddy, it's OK.

JEN. I am so proud of you, Will. You are glorious!

LILY. You are beautiful.

WILL. Alex, thank you. *The Da Vinci Code* revealed the secret truth of my life.

ALEX. My pleasure, Will.

WILL. I vote we keep the professor.

JEN & LILY. Yeah!

WILL. TEAM ALEX!

ANA. No! Will—please … don't—

ROB. Will, did you just smell the flower of life?

WILL. Yes! And I must smell some more.

ANA. I hate that Edith Wharton book!

WILL. Rob, buddy, we should read your book!

ANA. What?

ROB. My book?

WILL. Yes, let's read *Return of Tarzan*.

ANA. No!

ROB. Really? You would do that for me?

JEN, LILY & WILL. Yes!

ROB. Thanks.

ALEX. *Return of Tarzan* it is!

LILY. Wow.

JEN. I'm so happy for you, Will.

WILL. Thank you!

ROB. I'm so weirdly happy too. Aren't you, Ana?

ANA. Of course … I always knew. I mean … it's so obvious.

LILY. But Ana you always thought Will was still in love with you!

ALEX. Really?

WILL. Ana?

ANA. You must have all misunderstood me.

LILY. Ana, you said Will loved you. *(Whispers.)* It's on film.

(ANA looks at the camera.)

WILL. Ana, I wanted to believe that too, But the secret truth is—it was always Rob.

ANA *(beat)*. I think I need to lie down.

ROB. Are you feeling OK?

ANA. My chest … it feels funny.

(She exits, and ROB follows her out.)

WILL. God have mercy, I'm gay.

JEN. Oh Will, I've been waiting for this day for so long!

(JEN and WILL hug and weep.)

WILL *(cries)*. I'm so happy!

ALEX. Is Book Club always like this?

LILY. Absolutely!

(Lights shift.

***Projection:* Carl Banks, Book Dealer, Bay State Correctional Center, Framington, Massachusetts**.

Played by PUNDIT or ALEX in an orange jumpsuit.)

CARL. Here in the big house. We have a different sort of currency. Long days here, in the joint. And everyone is looking for some kind of release.

They call me "The Bookend." It goes like this. First three chapters, I am able to provide for free. You like that and want more, well … the next three will cost you three cigs.

Hooked and need another fix? Well chapters seven to nine will be a whole pack. And the book junkies … they come and beg for the last chapters. Ha! That's where the price jacks up to full chocolate bar. And that's when the craziness begins, the begging, the threats, the altercations. Shoot, one punk is in solitary today for perpetrating on my person to cut me if I didn't tell him the ending to *Presumed Innocent* by Scott Turow.

I protect myself and I do not read one word from those books. It's simple freakenomics. If you want to stay safe … never dabble in what you deal.

(Projection: **The Return of Tarzan By Edgar Rice Burroughs***.)*

ANA. Everyone, I want to apologize for my … resistance the last couple of get togethers. I want to be better and stronger than that. And I will be.

JEN. Ana, it's OK. You don't have to apologize to us.

ANA. But I do. You know, I think I was a little naïve when I said that all of this, the camera, the extra reading … wouldn't have an effect on us.

LILY. We've read a lot of books.

JEN. Yes.

ANA. And good books. Mostly. But I will be the first to admit that there were moments in the last weeks when I wasn't enjoying Book Club AT ALL. But I got an email from Lars Knudsen that he is really delighted with what he has seen so far.

ROB. Delighted?

ANA. Yes, he said Book Club was surprisingly "juicy."

(JEN and ROB look at each other in panic.)

JEN. Oh God. Did he talk about editing things out?

ANA. On the contrary; he wants more.

(Panicked, JEN and ROB, behind ANA and the rest of the Book Club's back, secretly signal to LARS to cut things.)

LILY *(she claps)*. Fabulous! Let's give Lars more. Sundance, here we come!

ANA. We'll see. And Alex, Lars specifically told me to thank you for your release.

ALEX *(to the camera)*. No. Thank you, Lars Knudsen.

ANA. He is planning on wrapping this all up in the next two or three sessions.

ROB *(dispirited)*. Awesome.

LILY. That soon? I think it's been kinda fun having old Lars with us.

ANA. Well, I for one will be grateful for all of us to return to our everyday, lovely normal lives and start having Book Club like it was.

JEN. Me too.

LILY. Ana, you are human, like the rest of us.

ANA. So human, really. I am. And Alex, I want to extend a personal apology to you.

ALEX. You do?

ANA. I'm just a little territorial; I am so deeply loyal to my Book Club family. I am afraid I may have come across as a tad unfriendly.

ALEX. I didn't notice.

ANA. We both know that I was a little protective.

ALEX. Apology accepted, Anuh-banana.

(ANA laughs and abruptly stops.)

ANA. Please don't.

ROB. Where is Will?

JEN. He just texted me. He should be here any minute.

ANA. Rob, I want you to know that I read this Tarzan book. Cover to cover … for you.

ROB. Ana, thank you.

JEN. I read it too.

LILY. Me too.

ALEX. So did I.

ROB. Wow. You read it? All of it? I'm amazed … all of you read it. The first book made such an impact on me. So … what … did you think!

(WILL enters in his Brooks Brothers suit. He looks the same and yet …)

ANA. Oh Will—how are you?

WILL. I'm a completely changed man, Ana. And better than ever. Thank you for asking,

ANA. I'm sorry I didn't join you all for lunch. I just was … I was trying to write.

WILL. We missed you. But it was a great lunch.

ALEX. Delicious.

ANA. Alex, you went too?

ALEX. I did.

ROB. After, we took Will shopping to places I never knew existed.

WILL. Me neither.

LILY. The Pleasure Chest. Egor's Dungeon, Good Vibrations.

ANA. Oh, my.

WILL. Lily was the one that knew where they were.

ALEX. Lily knows everything.

LILY. Not everything, not yet.

WILL. It was wonderful. *(Pulls out a necklace out from under his button-down shirt.)* But I just bought this rainbow necklace.

ANA. Oh.

WILL. Can I tell you, my beloved Book Club … how it feels to turn the page and start a whole new chapter in my life?

ROB. How does it feel?

WILL. Liberating! There is a whole world out there … waiting for you … if you just go and look for it.

JEN. And then Will's parents came into town and joined us for dinner.

ANA. Oh. Lunch. Shopping. And dinner?

LILY. Your mom is so funny.

WILL. She loves to laugh.

JEN. Omigod, Mr. Nothnagel was so … emotional.

ANA. It must be a little difficult for your father to comes to terms with—

ALEX. "The day you know who you truly are is the day you become a true man."

WILL. That's my pops.

LILY. It was so sweet.

ROB. I wish my parents were half as … connected … to me.

WILL. My parents love you.

ROB. Thanks.

WILL. You are my brother, Rob.

ROB. You're my bro too.

JEN & LILY. Aww! Bromance!

WILL. I don't know how I would have survived all these years without your straight-forward honesty and your friendship.

ROB. Thanks, bro.

WILL. And can I tell you? No matter how hard, you should always tell the truth. It will set you free and lead you to happiness.

ROB *(beat. Maybe ROB strongly hugs WILL in appreciation and confesses)*. I didn't read *Return of Tarzan*. I'm sorry. I couldn't get through it.

ANA. Rob, you didn't read the book you picked?

ROB. Tarzan was nothing like I remembered. I guess I'm not fifteen years old anymore!

ANA. You didn't read *Return of Tarzan*?

ROB. No, honey.

ANA. Rob!

ROB. And there's something else, Ana.

ANA. What?

ROB. I turned down the promotion.

ANA. You turned down the vice president promotion? Why?

ROB. Being a V.P. is not who I want to be … at all.

ANA. Rob?

ROB. And Ana: I kissed Jen.

ANA. WHAT?!!!

JEN. Oh God.

ROB. I kissed Jen.

LILY. Whoa.

WILL. Um, buddy.

ANA. You kissed Jen?

ALEX. Oh boy.

ANA. What? When?

ROB. During Book Club … After *The Age of Innocence.*

ANA. During my Book Club. How?

ROB. I just leaned over … and kissed her.

ALEX. On the lips?

ANA. Alex! What are you doing in this conversation?

ROB. I kissed her. On the lips.

JEN. Ana, it was … nothing!

ANA. Jen. What is it with you and married men!

ROB. This is not Jen's fault.

ANA. I am your wife, Rob.

ROB. I was confused, and Jen is a good friend … but this happened because of us.

ANA. So this is our fault?

ROB. No. It's mine. I've done what was expected of me because it was easier than figuring out what I wanted. I want the flower of life. I want to grow. I want to try new things. And I think you do too. Ana, my "Age of Innocence" is over.

ANA. Oh my God. That friggin' book …

ROB. Ana, I'm sorry.

ANA. Sorry?! Sorry?! You read one book for Book Club and you're confused? Rob, you are my husband who kissed my friend Jen. Jen, you kissed my husband and brought that idiot into my Book Club. Will, my first love, you decide to re-write our entire history. And you all did it in my Book Club at my house! On camera! In front of everybody! Have you no sense? Have you no respect? Have you no manners? Lily, you are the only true blue person here.

LILY. Ana, I need to tell you something. The *Herald* wants to attract a younger, hipper, more *urbane* audience. Ana, they offered me the Friday column.

ANA. My Friday column? You are taking over my Connections column?

LILY. I wanted you to hear it from me ... Ana, I'm so sorry.

ANA. You don't even like paper, you talented, little freak.

LILY. It's not personal.

ANA. It's personal to me! *(Stunned.)* You are my Book Club.

ROB. Ana—are you ... OK?

ANA. Jesus H. Christ! No, Rob! I'm not OK! What is wrong with you people! Turn off that camera!

JEN. Ana, we can't!

ANA. Take it down! Take it down! Oh God. This is too much! Nobody can see this!

WILL. We can't stop the camera.

ANA. Cover it! Cover it!'

(ANA grabs a blanket and throws it over the camera. The stage goes dark for a couple of seconds. In the dark:)

ANA *(cont'd)*. Arghh! I want to smash that machine!!

JEN. Ana, no!

WILL. Not the vase!

ANA. Lars, you've ruined my life. You've ruined my Book Club.

ROB. Ana!

LILY. Careful!

ANA. Lars, I hate you, I hate your film.

(ANA yells, out of control.)

ALL. Ana!

(Lights back on: ALEX is holding the blanket that was covering the camera. The room is in disarray. WILL, LILY, JEN and ROB are all holding ANA. ALEX sits and watches.)

ANA. Oh sweet Jesus! This is not the way Book Club is supposed to be!!!

WILL. Ana, you have to promise you will calm down.

ANA. I promise.

ROB. You have to control yourself.

ALEX. Book Club is like *Lord of the Flies* with wine and dip.

ANA. I am Ana Smith. I am Ana Smith. I'm … OK. I am always in control.

(They let go of her. She's sniffling, but getting herself together. She looks around at everyone).

ANA *(cont'd)*. I have something I want to show you.

(She walks out of the room and comes back holding a manuscript).

ANA *(cont'd)*. This is my book. My first three chapters.

ROB. You are writing a book?

WILL. About what?

ANA. All of you, even that jerk over there *(Points to ALEX.)* … have become more than my family, you have become a part of me. And this is my beautiful homage to what we had. *(Ceremoniously places the manuscript on the table.)* But I can't finish it … because the people I love and thought I knew … I don't know you anymore.

ROB. Ana, wait!

(ANA exits. Everyone is stunned ... ALEX goes up to the manuscript and picks it up.)

ALEX. Ana's book is called *The Book Club*.

JEN. *The Book Club*?

ALEX. Ana has written a book … about all of us.

LILY. What!? No!

JEN. She can't do that!

WILL. She wouldn't!

ROB. She did.

LILY *(beat)*. What should we do?

ALEX. We should read it.

JEN. No!

ROB. I'm not sure that's what Ana wants us to do.

WILL. For once, I don't know if even Ana knows what Ana wants.

JEN. What is the worst thing reading this book could do?

LILY *(pause)*. I'll go get photocopies.

ALEX. Lily?

LILY. Yes?

ALEX. I can't wait to read your column.

LILY. Thank you, Alex. *(Exits.)*

JEN. We should buy pizza and wine.

WILL. Let's go. I'll drive.

ROB. Don't worry. We will be right back!

(ROB, JEN and WILL exit.

ALEX watches them leave, then looks at the camera.)

ALEX. Who the hell are these people? And why do I like them so much?

(Lights shift.

Projection: Mrs. Edith P. Simpson, Retired Librarian, High Point, North Carolina.

Spotlight on EDITH [played by PUNDIT or LILY]. Wind is blowing. She is wearing goggles and a helmet and is about to jump out of a plane.)

MRS. SIMPSON. I am Mrs. Simpson. And today I am thrilled to be learning to sky dive.

Old Librarians can be crazy that way.

I am delighted to give you chickadees two little bits of advice.

One: read books. Real books. Books you can hold in your hand and carry in your head and your heart. My life has been decorated by every one of my foster kids and by every book I've ever read. In fact, yesterday, after sixty-two years of trying, I finally finished reading *Ulysses* by James Joyce.

Which brings me to my second bit of advice which is this: Get off your ass and do something with what you read. Because reading about life is not the same as living your life. Not the same at all. WHEEEEE! *(Jumps.)*

(Projection: The Book Club by Ana Smith.

Everybody is reading in different positions. Pizza boxes, wine and paper plates are everywhere.)

WILL. Unbelievable!

(WILL is done with his book. He is stunned. He puts the manuscript on the table.)

JEN. Good God Jupiter. Are you done already?

WILL. Yes. I'm done.

ROB. Well.

WILL. Keep reading.

(Everybody dives back in. WILL takes a drink.

LILY gasps then laughs.)

LILY. Oh no she did not.

(JEN paces as she flips pages.)

ROB. What?

LILY. Keep reading.

JEN. Oh my God. Oh My God!

ROB. Are you done?

JEN. OH MY GOD!

WILL. Have some wine.

LILY. All of that? In just three chapters?

ROB. OH! OH! OH!

(He reads through the climax to the last sentence. He closes the book and throws the book down.)

WILL. I know. Right?

(Everyone is done except ALEX. They all wait for him. ALEX calmly turns the last page.)

WILL. Alex?

ALEX. Done.

WILL. So?

ROB. Wow. That was intense.

JEN. I don't know what to say—

LILY. It's terrible and untrue.

ROB. Not all of it.

WILL. Enough of it.

WILL. She never told us she was writing about us!

JEN. She used our Book Club!

LILY. Everything we did and said in Book Club is in here!

JEN. It's amazing. And terrible.

LILY. It's like it's me … but it's not me. I know I said these things, but is that really who I am? I'm confused.

ROB. Me too! I don't know what to think.

ALEX. One thing is for sure: This book is going to sell! It is so … Ana. Smart and driven. Earnestly writing about friendship and food and books.

JEN. But our Book Club isn't really like this.

(ANA opens the door.)

ANA. Oh. I didn't think you all would still be here.

ROB. Are you all right, honey?

ANA. Of course I am, Rob. What a mess.

JEN. I'll say. Hi, Ana.

ANA. I'm sorry everything got so … uncomfortably intense.

ROB. Are you feeling better now?

ANA. I don't know.

WILL. Why don't you sit down?

(WILL rights an overturned chair for her. She sits.)

LILY. Ana, we read your book.

ANA. Oh! You did?

ALEX. We all did.

JEN. Yup, sure did.

ANA. It's only the first three chapters.

WILL. It's more than enough.

ANA. Oh. Thank you. It wasn't easy to write.

ROB. It wasn't easy to read, honey.

ALEX. Oh, I disagree. This is fun!

"Ann's beautiful green eyes swept the room. Truth be known, in her lesser moments, Ann would selfishly dream of running away and releasing herself from the burden of her friends' unfulfilled lives. But she never would abandon her Book Club … "

ANA. Writing a book is harder than I thought. I've poured my heart and soul into this.

LILY. Why didn't you tell us you were writing a book about our Book Club?

ANA. It's really not so much about you all.

JEN. "Ann's heart burned with compassion for Jan. Poor Jan was a woman of *promise* who had been eroded by her predatory 'hussy' tendencies. She could have been a judge or an astronaut, but instead, Jan had flittered her life away, shuffling other people's papers and dreaming of tasting the lips of men who would never love her."

ANA. In so many ways, Jan is the heroine of the story.

LILY. "Ann's gaze fell upon beautiful and vibrant Lula. It was clear the smarmy professor Alvin was smitten with Lula. He was a dangerous, vulgar man. Lula was utterly alone; her mother had long vanished into the sepulchral haze of crack cocaine. Ann knew she would have to mother where another had failed.

ANA. Lily, you are a writer and editor. You realize this is a rough rough first draft.

WILL. "She could not help but wonder if she had chosen rightly. Would Phil not have been the perfect husband? The most devoted father? Phil's furtive looks her way filled her with despair. That the love had never died was undeniable … and yet … despite his nobility, there was something decidedly frumpy about Phil.

ROB. "And there was Bob. A college football quarterback, who had tackled Ann's senses with his sweet smile and steely abs. Ann knew Bob was a man with the soul of a poet trapped in the body of an all-American. Ann knew in her heart that he would always be there for her, even if he wasn't there for himself."

ANA. Ann loves Bob so much.

ROB. My name isn't Bob. And my abs are not so steely.

JEN. Ana! You can't just invent things about us.

WILL. Frumpy Phil is not me! In or out of the closet!

ANA. Guys! Guys!

LILY. I'm not a poor girl from the ghetto. My parents are dentists!

JEN. We're people, Ana. Not characters.

ANA. This is fiction, people! It's called literary license. You are my friends and you inspired these characters. You are complex and interesting people in my living room, but the truth is you are not compelling enough to be characters in a book. That's all.

ALEX. Ana is right. A pot boiler must boil over.

ANA. I didn't mean to hurt any of you. It's just a book. These are just characters …

ALEX. "Just characters"? Think of it! There are billions of human beings that have passed through this earth, and the ones we remember the best, the ones that last: Scarlett O'Hara, Jane Eyre, Don Quixote, Heathcliff, well … they never existed. We live and we die and the matter of our daily lives evaporates the moment it happens. Except a part of us will live on, every time someone reads this book.

LILY. Ana, how does *The Book Club*—no—how does your book end? What happens to the rest of us? I mean them.

ANA. Well, I think Lula, she rises too quickly in her job … and finds herself successful but very alone.

LILY. Oh hell, no! It's not fair for Lula to be lonely for that long.

JEN. And what happens to Jan?

ROB. And Bob?

WILL. And Phil?

ALEX. Ana, what happens to the character of Ann?

ANA. I don't know. I'm stuck. And so are they. Those characters aren't developing into who I thought they would be. You know. This is all Lars Knudsen's fault. That bug-eyed camera changed everything. It made us self-conscious and intensely uncomfortable. Everyone, let's walk out right now, away from the judgmental eye of the camera, and continue our meeting at Starbucks. I'm sorry Lars Knudsen, but I must protect my Book Club.

WILL. It's *our* Book Club, Ana. OUR Book Club. And it was MY idea to start it!

ANA. OK! OK! It was your idea.

JEN. We are Book Club. We are a group!

ANA. Yes, and I am the glue of this group.

JEN. Ana, you are an amazing and strong woman. People like you run the world from PTAs to Congress. The world needs people like you.

ANA. Thank you, Jen.

JEN. But sometimes, people like you break things and you don't know it. You used our Book Club without our permission. Book Club is not ours anymore … it's just you. Ana … our Book Club is broken.

ANA. Book Club is broken?

WILL. Ana, our Book Club is done.

(ANA absorbs the painful news.)

ANA. My book broke Book Club?

ROB *(beat)*. Yes it did, honey.

ANA. Oh—Now I know what happens to the character of Ann: she loses everything.

ROB *(earnest)*. That's beautiful and tragic, honey.

ANA *(sinks to the floor)*. It's times like this when it really sucks being an overachiever. Who needs Book Club? Who needs to be social? Hell, who needs the inconvenience of having living breathing people in their living room? Well … I do. I need you. I love you.

(She cries and falls apart.)

ANA *(cont'd)*. Please forgive me. I never thought my book would hurt you. I'm so sorry. *(To ROB but it's too painful.)* What am I going to do without you? Without my Book Club?

(Beat. WILL picks up the manuscript.)

WILL. Ana, you still have *your* Book Club.

LILY. Ana—You really should finish writing your book.

ANA. Really?

JEN. Yes, it was a painful, but a really good read.

ANA. Oh I would if I could … *(Beat.)* But … how should I end it all for these people? Sorry. These characters.

ALEX *(hands it to her)*. Any way you want, Ana. You are the author.

ANA. Right …

ALEX. You're in charge. You're in total control.

ANA *(beat)*. You're right. *(Beat.)* I'm the author. I'm in charge. *(Tentative.)* And in total control of this Book Club. Thank you, Alex! Beloved Book Club, I so appreciate your encouragement. I will go to Starbucks to write my Book Club book right now. *(Beat.)* You know, Rob, honey, I know it ruined everything … and I know it wasn't fun for you, but thank you for reading my book.

(ROB walks up to her.)

ROB. Ana, you are most complicated and infuriating woman I know.

(He kisses her passionately.)

ROB *(cont'd)*. You are the flower of my life.

ANA. Rob. Wow.

ROB. We have a lot to talk about. But now go write your book at Starbucks.

ANA. Thank you, honey. I really want to write this book. And then I have get it published. And then, if I am lucky, I can sell the rights to make it into a movie.

ROB. A movie!!

ANA. Or a play.

(Everyone looks at each other less enthused about the play idea.)

ROB. Now is the right time, Ana.

ANA *(kisses him)*. Rob, you are my Tarzan, always. *(To all.)* Everyone, please clean up before I come back.

(ANA leaves.)

LILY. Alex, would you like to go to the opera or a poetry slam with me sometime?

ALEX. Lily, I would like that very much, thank you.

JEN. Will, will you have a baby with me?

WILL. What?

JEN. I don't want to interfere with your new life but would you father a child for me?

WILL *(delighted)*. Kids?! With me?

ROB. You'd be great parents.

WILL. A little Nothnagel in the world? Me? A pop? My parents will be so shocked. I would be honored, Jenny.

JEN. Thank you, Will.

ROB. I can't believe Book Club is breaking up.

LILY. I know, I am going to miss you all.

WILL. Me too. I am truly going to miss Book Club.

ALEX. What if one of YOU starts a new Book Club?

JEN. I can lead Book Club! Totally!

LILY. It can be a potluck!

JEN & LILY. Yes!

WILL. Oh! Can I join?

JEN. Of course!

ROB. I would like to come too.

WILL. Rob, really?!

ROB. Book Club is good for me.

JEN. Awesome!

ALEX. Can I come?

JEN. Yes, Alex.

ALEX. Awesome times two!

LILY. So this is our new Book Club!!!

ROB. Could I pick the book?

ALL. Yes.

ROB. I'm ready for something … epic. Where characters love and lose and grow. I want to travel to a land I've never seen and get to know people I've never met … and then feel at the end, that they are a part of me and my life

JEN. Yeah!

ALEX. Oh. We should read *War and Peace.*

LILY. Alex, That's an inspired choice.

ROB. Yeah! Let's read *War and Peace.*

WILL. All right, buddy!

LILY. Rob, I think it's more than a thousand pages.

JEN. Really? A thousand pages.

ROB. Oh … perfect!!

(Lights out.

Epilogue. Lights up on:)

ANA. My book *The Book Club* is a huge bestseller that's being made into a film by Martin Scorsese. More importantly, Rob and I are taking a really big new step by adopting a beautiful baby …

ROB. Gorilla … that lives in a wildlife preserve in Kenya! After reading *Wuthering Heights*, I totally want to call him Heathcliff!

WILL. You know, I read Dan Brown's other books and I did not like them. *The Da Vinci Code*, well … it was the right book at the right time. Some books just turn you upside down … and suddenly you can see the world right side up.

JEN. Will is a wonderful father to our two twin girls: Charlotte and Emily and is dating a former Secret Service agent who loves Ernest Hemingway. I've gone back to law school! And I'm in the top of my class! And I still lose my keys all the time.

LILY. Book Club has been really good for me. Losing myself in a good book is like taking a journey. And finding someone who has read the same book is like finding a true soul mate on a lonely road.

ALEX. I got tenure at the university and celebrated by getting down on one knee and proposing.

LILY. I said, "Yes."

ALEX. God, *(Looks at LILY.)* I love … Book Club!

(All actors take a bow and exit.

Projection: IN MEMORIAM

Beat.

Projection: Edith P. Simpson, Librarian,

Beat.

Projection: Sky-Diving Casualty

The following list is aslo projected:

The Book Club Reading List (Books Cited):
Moby Dick
Sounder
Old Yeller

Tarzan of the Apes
The Little House
Wuthering Heights
Paradise Lost
The Age of Innocence
Love in the Time of Cholera
Black Like Me
Native Son
The Color Purple
Beloved
Devil in a Blue Dress
Twilight
Fifty Shades of Grey
Ulysses
Search for Love
The Da Vinci Code
The Hunger Games
Harry Potter
Chicken Soup for the Soul
Lolita
Return of Tarzan
Charlotte's Web
Lord of the Flies
Gone With The Wind
Jane Eyre
Don Quixote of la Mancha
War and Peace
and
The Book Club
By Ana Smith
(A *New York Times* Bestseller)

NOTES